By KAREEN ZEBROFF
and PETER ZEBROFF

Drawings by Lo Linkert

STERLING PUBLISHING CO., INC. NEW YORK
Oak Tree Press Co., Ltd. Sydney

OTHER BOOKS OF INTEREST

Better Roller Skating

Body-Building and Self-Defense

Dancing Games for Children of
 All Ages

Girls' Gymnastics

Gymnastics

Junior Judo

Junior Karate

Junior Tennis

Karate for Young People

Movement Games for Children of All
 Ages

ACKNOWLEDGMENTS

Our sincere thanks to all the children who helped in the production of this book: Barbara, Darrell and Sandra Achtem, Angela Dodds, Emily Erickson, Malcolm and Sharon McDougall, Eric Slocum, Konia and Licia Trouton, Petra, Tanya and Sylvie Zebroff.

DEDICATION

To our children and yours for
better health and happiness

Photographs by Duncan McDougall

Originally published under the title "Yoga with Your Children"
© 1973 by Fforbez Enterprises Ltd., Vancouver, B.C., Canada

WHAT'S IN
THIS BOOK?

FOREWORD TO PARENTS

This book is written for children. We speak expressly to them. Now and then, we need your help, however, to organize a personal program just right for *your* child. Yoga is non-competitive and therefore provides a high degree of pleasure and success to even the least athletic. It also gives joy to the gifted child because there is always a more advanced stage to work towards. As you work out a Personal Yoga Schedule or exercise plan with your offspring you may find him to be surprisingly inflexible for his age. We can safely say that at least one of the authors is more flexible than the average 7 year old. To us that seems shocking and sad. Our more sedentary, T.V.-oriented life is obviously to blame. But — it is not too late. Tightened muscles *can* be stretched; a crimped spine can be loosened; balance and poise can be regained.

Your first step consists of carefully reading the section on SCHEDULES. Make a list of poses your child could benefit from by consulting the *Schedules for Health Problems* (ignore it if your lucky child has none of the listed ones) or by looking at the *Schedules for Specific Areas* to either strengthen a weak back, build up the biceps or develop a bigger bust. In short, for your child's sake read the whole book so that you can explain to him the essence of successful and "fun" yoga exercising: personal, non-competitive progress; slow movement; holding positions; the use of imagination, which will enhance the concentration; proper breathing; the history and the "how, when, where, who, and why -to" of it all. As the best educating is always done by example, why not join your little love in gently rolling about the floor while almost incidentally improving your health, beauty and peace of mind as well. In our automated hectic world, even children need relaxing. If that is not food for thought, what is?

K.H.Z. & P.W.Z. September, 1973

KIDS . . . YOGA CAN BE FUN

Do you like to play "let's pretend" or "follow-the-leader"? If you do, then Yoga is for you because that's what we do a lot of the time in Yoga. It all started about 5000 years ago when some wise men in ancient India decided that they wanted to become as relaxed and flexible and alert as the cat families of the jungle. They watched and copied these big cats and noticed that their movements were almost all stretching ones. You see, the work of the muscles is to contract (tighten) — that's all they do. Some muscles contract to help you bend forward, others to bend backward. When they work too hard or when you are uptight about something, the muscles tighten even more and pretty soon they have forgotten how to let go. That is why some people can't bring their hands to the floor or their heads to their knees — their hamstring muscles at the back of their legs are too tight! If you decide to stretch them by a lot of fast toe-touches, you may hurt the muscles and they will be sore the next day. But if you stretch them gently with Yoga poses, by going as far as you can and NO FURTHER, and holding that position for awhile, your muscles will slowly learn to relax and in a few days or weeks you will be much more flexible. You will surprise yourself. No pain, but lots of results. Remember though, you must hold until it gets uncomfortable the first time. One second longer the next time.

The old Yogis found that with the "animal exercises" they felt a lot better — they could run faster, sleep better, jump higher and had lots of energy to do their chores. Their bodies would be so relaxed that they could sit still for several hours in order to meditate. They taught these wonderful exercises to their children who taught it to theirs and for 2500 years they were passed on by word of mouth. Then a man, Patanjali, put it all in writing with special Indian (Sanskrit) names. Some of the names were chosen according to which animal the pose was copied from or which animals they most looked like. If you pretend to be a cat when you do the Cat Stretch, it will, of course help you to do it better. The pictures and cartoons should give you ideas for pretending while you exercise. While you have fun imagining that you are a lioness looking for her little cubs or that you are a little cub playing in front of the cave, you will be getting many benefits from the exercises.

SCHEDULES

PLANNING A SCHEDULE

— What type of exercise do I need?
— Do I have any health problems?
— Have I considered all the benefits?
— What should my personal Yoga schedule include?
— When should I exercise?
— Where is the best place to do Yoga?

Schedules for health problems

Schedules for different parts of the body

PLANNING JUST FOR YOU

YOU are an individual. Your body has vastly different characteristics and needs from everybody else. For instance, you may be a person who was born with a wide scope to your hip-socket, so that you can do the difficult lotus posture the first time you try it. Your best friend may have to work at it unsuccessfully for years. But if he can eat all the sugary, sweet foods he likes without gaining weight, whereas you break out in spots and/or gain pounds after a few candies or a piece of lemon-meringue pie — you may be sure that he was born with 2,000,000 islands on his pancreas whereas you have only 200,000. So you can see that your friend's body and what he needs to do with it differs greatly from your own. And nobody can make up a better schedule for it than you or your parents since they know you pretty well. There are many questions you have to take into consideration when you plan your own, personalized YOGA SCHEDULE:

1. WHAT TYPE OF EXERCISE DO I NEED?
   a) Consult your doctor and see if your weight is normal compared to your height. If it is much higher or much lower, concentrate on exercises that REGULATE the function of the thyroid gland (weight regulator of the body), with such poses as the SHOULDERSTAND, PLOW, and FISH.
   b) Practice some balancing poses with your eyes closed to see if your sense of balance, which controls graceful movement, posture, poise and even athletic performance, is good. If you totter almost immediately do lots of balancing poses and stand on one leg whenever you can during the day, for example, on the phone. Balance 'tone' must be worked on as much as muscle tone.
   c) Gently try a few poses from the book and you'll see very quickly whether you are flexible or how good your muscle tone is. Probably you'll be horrified at how stiff you are already at your young age. Don't feel discouraged —unfortunately this is true of most young people nowadays. Most schools simply do not have the time nor the facilities to keep growing muscles and bones like yours sufficiently exercised. For greater fun, better weight and health and better looks all round, you need the extra-curricular activity of Yoga.

2. DO I HAVE ANY HEALTH PROBLEMS?

a) Have your doctor give you a check-up and take into consideration any identifiable health problem such as diabetes, sway back, epilepsy, fallen arches, etc.

b) Now look under the SCHEDULE FOR HEALTH PROBLEMS, find the heading that applies to you and try out all the poses listed. Don't panic — you don't have to do all these, just one or two, that you feel are best for YOU. Mind you, these are not necessarily the easiest ones, but they should be what "grab you most."

3. HAVE I CONSIDERED ALL THE BENEFITS?

a) Not only do we all have different needs but body build also varies greatly from person to person. There are three distinct types from big-boned and tall, to small-boned and short with variations in between. ALL THESE ARE BEAUTIFUL! There is no use bemoaning your type and wishing for the opposite, because tastes are different as well. To someone you will seem beautiful no matter what your build, IF you are proportionate. This means that nothing must be outsize or undersize for that matter. This is where Yoga Exercise comes in. It can help to reduce or to develop. Beauty lies in proportion, because that is pleasing to the eye. Stand in front of a mirror and decide first of all that you are basically beautiful — with a little room for improvement in perhaps the: shoulders, chest, bust, biceps, hips, calves or whatever. Put on some comfortable exercising clothes, such as shorts or tights and tee shirt.

b) NOW go to the BENEFITS sections and carefully read them for all the exercises. Check, and make a note of each exercise that hits you where the trouble spot lies. Oversize buttocks — aha, the Locust will help to take care of that. Puny Chest? — the Chest Expander and Cobra are fantastic for such problems.

4. WHAT SHOULD MY PERSONAL YOGA SCHEDULE INCLUDE?

a) WARM-UP — this is *absolutely essential* — because without it you will get hurt. No good mechanic would think of running the car without first idling it. In Yoga there are none of the usual muscular aches, because of warm-ups and slow movement.

b) THREE OR FOUR OR MORE POSES chosen by you, just for you from the HEALTH PROBLEM section to keep YOU fit and well. Try to plan these to include at least one forward bending pose, one backward bending, one twisting, one balancing, one side bending pose, depending, of course, on your needs. If your balance is exceptionally good, for example, you could substitute a problem pose for a balancing one.

c) AN INVERTED POSE — should always be included in any balanced schedule. It will: improve the circulation; make you more alert and lively; and work on your "inner" health. A good time to do these poses is just after the warm-up while you are still fresh, so that you can hold the inverted pose longer. Work up slowly to holding it at least 3 minutes or more by starting with 30 seconds and adding 5 seconds a day. But while you are up there you can "fool around," by putting your legs, ankles and feet into all sorts of different positions, holding each for awhile. The Headstand, however, is an advanced pose and the neck, arms, shoulders, back and abdomen all have to be strong before it is attempted. You must concentrate on strengthening your weak areas and practicing the Headstand Attempt for a few weeks or months.

d) End your exercising with a RELAXATION POSE — to let your body have a chance to absorb what it has just been taught. Also, muscles that have been tense because of neglect and are now being stretched to relax them, will appreciate a short rest after their work-out.

e) A BREATHING EXERCISE — is without doubt the most important part of your Personal Yoga Schedule. Oxygen is your most important body-food. You can do without eating for over a month but without air for only 4 minutes. Your body renews itself inside out every seven years. You have not one of the same cells you had when you were small. Oxygen is needed by the brain for its computer work, by the blood to carry to every part of the body for cell repair. After you have learned to breathe properly with Yoga you should make a point of breathing deeply for about 10 minutes a day. This need not be done at the exercising time but when you are outdoors or in a just-aired room with the windows now shut. You'll be surprised at how energetic a little breathing can make you feel. Try it.

Talk your selections over with Mom or Dad and explain why you are doing each pose.

Sample Program

1 Warm-up	Cat Stretch
1 Health Problem or Balancing Pose	Stork
1 Keep Fit Exercise	Headstand
1 Beauty Pose	Forward Bend
1 Favorite Pose	Camel
1 Breathing	Cooling Breath
1 Relaxation Pose	Sponge

Great! Now you have a plan just for you—the perfect one. Adjust it as you go along and ALWAYS remember the Yoga principle of slow movement, a holding position, proper breathing with each pose, individual slow or fast progress and positive thinking.

5. WHEN SHOULD I EXERCISE?

It is suggested you should never exercise after eating. You should always empty your bladder and bowels, as well as blowing your nose before starting Yoga exercises.

6. WHERE IS THE BEST PLACE TO DO YOGA?

A quiet place is best because you can concentrate, count and keep records more easily. You can do this in the bedroom, empty recreation room, etc. or on the rug in front of the fire, on a small mat in the dining room or anywhere there is room to stretch your body. You can exercise in front of the television (preferably not there but if it will help you to get down and exercise — then do).

SCHEDULES FOR HEALTH PROBLEMS

ANEMIA:

Forward Bends, Complete Breath, Shoulderstand, Sponge.

ARTHRITIS:

Cobra, Cow Head Pose, Forward Bend, Shoulderstand, Triangle Posture, Locust, Twist, Curling Leaf.

ASTHMA:

Forward Bends, Cobra, Fish, Headstand, Locust, Warrior, Shoulderstand, Alternate Leg Stretch.

BACKACHE:

All standing poses, Bow, Cobra, Forward Bend, Shoulderstand, Alternate Leg Stretch, Reverse Arch.

BALANCE AND POISE:

Crow, Forward Bend, Leg Split, Stork.

COMMON COLD:

Both Forward Bends; Complete Breath, Headstand, Shoulderstand.

CONSTIPATION:

Forward Bends, Bow, Chest Expander, Fish, Headstand, Plow, Shoulderstand, Triangle Postures, Twist, Alternate Leg Stretch.

DIABETES:

Fish, Forward Bends, Locust, Peacock, Plow, Shoulderstand, Twist, Alternate Leg Stretch.

DIGESTION:

See Constipation and Indigestion.

DISPLACED DISC:

All Standing Postures, Bow, Camel, Cobra, Forward Bends, Locust, Shoulderstand, Cat Stretch.

FATIGUE:

Forward Bends, Chest Expander, Complete Breath, Headstand, Plow, Sun Salutations, Shoulderstand, Twist, Curling Leaf.

FLAT FEET:

Sitting and Reclining Warrior, Shoulderstand, Knee and Thigh Stretch.

GALL BLADDER:

Forward Bends, Locust, Shoulderstand, Triangle Postures, Twist, Alternate Leg Stretch.

GLANDS (endocrine, pituitary, pineal):

Headstand, Tortoise.

HEADACHE:

Alternate Nostril Breathing, Forward Bends, Headstand, Plow, Shoulderstand (for 3 mins. or more).

HEELS:

Shoulderstand, Sitting Warrior, Triangle Postures, Knee and Thigh Stretch.

HERNIA PREVENTION:

Spider.

INDIGESTION:

Ankle to Forehead Stretch, Bow, Cobra, Locust, Peacock, Plow, Shoulderstand.

INSOMNIA:

Alternate Nostril Breathing, Cobra, Forward Bends, Headstand, Plow, Shoulderstand, Sun Salutation.

KIDNEYS:

Bow, Cobra, Forward Bends, Locust, Plow, Shoulderstand, Tortoise, Knee and Thigh Stretch, Twist.

LUMBAGO:

Bow, Cobra, Locust, Plow, Sponge.

MENSTRUAL DISORDERS (PAIN AND IRREGULARITY) AND OVARIES:

Forward Bend, Cobra, Fish, Shoulderstand, Sitting and Reclining Warrior, Triangle Postures, Knee and Thigh Stretch, Cat Stretch, Reverse Arch.

PILES:

Bow, Fish, Locust (Boat), Plow, Shoulderstand.

RHEUMATISM:

Forward Bends, Plow, Reclining Warrior, Twist, Shoulderstand, Locust (Boat), Alternate Leg Stretch.

SINUS:

Headstand, Chest Expander.

SLIMMING:

Forward Bends, Cobra, Locust, Triangle Poses, Wheel, Bow, Fish, Plow, Shoulderstand, Twist, Fountain.

SLIPPED DISC:

See Displaced Disc.

TENSION:

Chest Expander, Cobra, Cow Head Pose, Forward Bends, Plow, Shoulderstand, Sun Salutation, Sponge, Twist, Lion, Fish, Rockn' Rolls, Alternate Leg Stretch, Curling Leaf.

12

SCHEDULES FOR DIFFERENT PARTS OF THE BODY

ABDOMEN:

Ankle to Forehead Stretch, Forward Bending, Bow, Chest Expander, Crow, Headstand, Locust, Lotus, Peacock, Plow, Sun Salutation, Tortoise, Alternate Leg Stretch, Rockn' Rolls.

ANKLES:

Cobra, Forward Bends, Lotus, Triangle, Postures, Wheel, Knee and Thigh Stretch, Sitting Warrior.

ARMS & WRISTS:

Ankle to Forehead Stretch, Bow, Chest Expander, Cobra, Cow Head Pose, Crow, Peacock, Cat Stretch, Fountain.

BACK & SPINE:

Bow, Chest Expander, Cobra, Forward Bends, Locust, Lotus, Plow, Tortoise, Twist, Wheel, Alternate Leg Stretch, Boat, Camel, Cat Stretch.

BUST & CHEST:

Bow, Chest Expander, Cobra, Cow Head Pose, Crow, Fish, Forward Bends, Plow, Sun Salutation, Wheel, Triangle Postures.

BUTTOCKS:

Bow, Cobra, Locust, Plow, Shoulderstand, Wheel, Alternate Leg Stretch.

CIRCULATION:

Chest Expander, Cow Head Pose, Dog Stretch, Forward Bends, Headstand, Peacock, Shoulderstand, Spider, Sun Salutation, Wheel, Curling Leaf.

EYES:

Headstand, Shoulderstand, Lion.

FACE:

Forward Bending, Plow, Shoulderstand, Lion.

FEET:

Forward Bending, Reclining Warrior.

13

HIPS:

Ankle to Forehead Stretch, Bow, Chest Expander, Leg Split, Plow, Shooting Bow, Spider, Triangle Posture, Twist, Locust, Fountain.

KNEES:

Forward Bending, Lotus, Twist, Alternate Leg Stretch, Knee and Thigh Stretch, Sitting Warrior.

LEGS:

Bow, Chest Expander, Cow Head Pose, Forward Bends, Leg Split, Reclining Warrior, Tortoise, Alternate Leg Stretch, Curling Leaf, Stork.

LUNGS: (see also ASTHMA)

Chest Expander, Headstand.

NECK & CHIN:

Chest Expander, Cobra, Crow, Fish, Plow, Cat Stretch.

PELVIC AREA:

Cobra, Locust, Reclining Warrior.

POSTURE & SHOULDERS:

Bow, Chest Expander, Cobra, Cow Head Pose, Forward Bends, Lotus, Plow, Camel, Stork.

THIGHS:

Ankle to Forehead Stretch, Eagle Pose, Forward Bends, Leg Split, Reclining Warrior, Spider, Triangle Posture, Wheel, Alternate Leg Stretch, Knee and Thigh Stretch.

WAIST & MIDRIFF:

Sun Salutation, Triangle Posture, Twist, Fountain.

WARM-UP POSES

Check each exercise for benefits.

Do at least one Warm-up Pose
before any other exercises
so that you don't strain or
pull any muscles.

After trying each Warm-up
select one and put it on
your Personal Yoga Schedule.

CAT STRETCH

Directions:

Pretend to be inside the warm, stretchy skin of a cat.
1. Kneel on all fours. (Figure 1)
2. Rocking slightly back first, INHALE and lower your chest in a sweeping motion, trying to rest the Adam's apple on the floor. (Figure 2)
3. Hold the position for 5 seconds, with most of the weight on the arms.
4. EXHALE, return to the first position and arch the back in an upward motion like an angry, spitting cat. (Figure 3)
5. Hold for 5 seconds, relax.
6. Now bring your right knee towards the head, and touch it if you can. Hold 5 seconds. (Figure 4)
7. Stretch the leg out and up in back, keeping it straight. Hold. Keep the head up and arms straight. (Figure 5)
8. Return the leg slowly to the head. Hold.
9. Relax. Repeat on the other side.
10. Repeat the whole series once or twice more.

Dos and Don'ts:

DO enjoy the stretching movement of your body. Move slowly and with grace.
DON'T be discouraged by not getting your knees to your head for awhile. With practice you'll improve quickly.

Benefits:

THE CAT STRETCH

•strengthens the back •reduces tension •strengthens the arms •helps to regulate menstrual periods •tightens the chin area •stretches the whole front of the body.

16

(Figure 1) Start on all fours.

(Figure 2) You're a pussycat lapping her milk.

(Figure 3) Someone stepped on your tail and you're mad.

(Figure 4) Touch your forehead if you can.

(Figure 5) Really stretch — somebody is pulling on your toes.

CHEST EXPANDER

Directions:

Pretend to be a muscleman working out before his open window.

1. Stand straight, feet slightly apart and bring arms forward, palms together. (Figure 6)
2. INHALE and bring the arms behind the back in a wide circling motion, knifing the shoulder blades together. Clasp the hands.
3. Letting your head fall back, bend backward as far as you comfortably can, *pushing the pelvis forward.*
4. Push the clasped hands up toward your head and hold this position for 5 seconds. (Figure 7)
5. Now, staying in the same position, EXHALE and bend slowly forward from the waist, letting the head hang down. Let your body weight pull you down, but do not jerk or bounce. (Figure 8)
6. Hold this position for 10 seconds and keep pushing the hands up towards the head. (Figure 9)
7. Straighten slowly, relax, and then repeat twice more.

Dos and Don'ts:

DON'T close your eyes, in order to keep your balance better.
DO push up on your hands without moving before bending forward.

Benefits:

THE CHEST EXPANDER

•builds the bust for the girls and expands the chest for the boys •acts as quick quick energizer •improves posture •firms and reduces a "layered" tummy •relaxes the whole body •expands the lungs and improves circulation to the head•relieves tension in the neck, shoulders and upper back

(Figure 6) Starting position.

(Figure 7) The arms have come back in a swimming motion.

(Figure 8) Don't cheat by bending your knees.

(Figure 9) If you can, bring your head to your knees.

19

ROCKN' ROLLS

Directions:

Pretend to be a ladybug having a "rock-in."

1. Sit on the floor, knees bent.
2. Clasp your hands under the knees.
3. Bring your head as close to the knees as possible and keep it there throughout. (Figure 10)
4. Rock gently back onto the spine, keeping the back rounded and the legs together. (Figure 11)
5. Establish an easy rhythm in rocking back and forth. (Figure 12)
6. Repeat 12 times or rock for 60 seconds.
7. Remember to breathe: in on the back rock, out on the forward rock.

Dos and Don'ts:

DO start the whole exercise on your back if you are a bit timid about rocking back from a sitting position. This way swing the lower legs up to get you going.

DO the Rockn' Rolls any time you want to get the kinks out of your body.

DO keep your head close to your knees, to have a rounded spine to rock on.

DO use the momentum of the first backward rock to return forward again.

Benefits:

THE ROCKN' ROLLS

•acts as an excellent warm-up and energizer •limbers up the spine •strengthens the abdominal muscles •massages and reduces tension in the neck and spine •is beneficial to the liver and spleen •aids digestion and elimination.

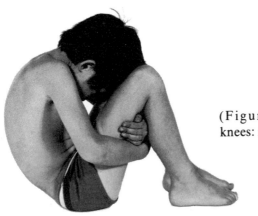

(Figure 10) Head to knees: now keep it there!

(Figure 11) Don't go too far — we want you back.

(Figure 12) Back and forth, easy and smooth.

21

SUN
SALUTATION

Directions:

Pretend to be a seal warming himself in the sun after an icy swim.

1. Stand with the feet slightly apart, the hands together in front of the chest. Take a couple of breaths. (Figure 13)
2. INHALE, raise the arms over the head and bend slowly backward from the waist, pushing the hips forward. (Figure 14)
3. EXHALE, bend forward and bring the hands to the floor beside the feet, keeping the knees straight. (Figure 15)
4. INHALE, squat and bring the right foot back, keeping the right knee straight. Keep the bottom down, raise the head and try to arch the back down. (Figure 16)
5. HOLD your breath and bring the left leg alongside the right one, keeping the body in a straight line (similar to a Push-up), with only the hands and toes supporting it. (Figure 17)
6. EXHALE and slowly lower the body to the floor in this order: knees, chest and forehead. (Figure 18)
7. INHALE and in a smooth motion lower the hips to the floor, at the same time raising the head and arching the back in a Cobra position. (Figure 19)
8. EXHALE, push down on the hands, stick the bottom way up, straightening the knees and pushing down on the heels. (Figure 20)
9. INHALE and bring the right foot forward setting it down between the hands. Keep the left leg extended, raise the head and arch the back down. (Figure 21)
10. EXHALE, bring the left leg forward, straighten the knees and perform a Forward Bend, the head as close to the knees as possible. (Figure 22)
11. INHALE, straighten up with the arms over the head and bend back again as far as you can go. (Figure 23)
12. EXHALE, come forward, lower the arms and relax. (Figure 24)
13. Repeat this cycle once more in smooth, fluid motions, this time bringing the left leg back first. Eventually work up to 12 repetitions.

Dos and Don'ts:

DO "PAUSE" for just a moment, rather than "HOLD" at the limit of each position.

DO think of your movements as rhythmic forward and backward motions of the spine. Enjoy the stretches.

DO remember the proper breathing.

DO raise the head and arch the back in steps 4 and 9. Keep the knee of the outstretched leg on the floor. Alternate legs.

To really feel the beauty of the wave-like motions in the Sun Salutation you should do them while watching the sun rise.

Benefits:

THE SUN SALUTATION POSE

●acts as an excellent energizer ●reduces weight in the waist and abdomen ●expands the chest and makes breathing easier ●makes the spine supple and healthy ●improves the circulation to the whole body ●prepares and strengthens the muscles for more advanced poses ●increases stamina ●relieves tension and insomnia.

(Figure 13)
Starting position.

(Figure 14) Think, stretching in the sunshine.

(Figure 15) Make a good effort but don't strain.

(Figure 16) The left thigh and calf come together.

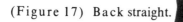

(Figure 17) Back straight.

(Figure 18) Head down, chest down, bottoms up!

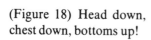

(Figure 19) Just like a cobra.

(Figure 20) Tuck the toes under, bring heels to the floor.

(Figure 21) The leg that went back before, now comes forward.

25

(Figure 22) Back to that forward bend position.

(Figure 23) Have a good stretch.

(Figure 24) Back where we started from.

EASY KEEP FIT
YOGA POSES

For beginners.

Easy exercises to keep fit.

Adults can do most of these.

A good refresher section for those returning to Yoga.

A gentle preparation for the more advanced stage.

Remember to go as far as *you* can and hold it there.

27

ALTERNATE LEG STRETCH

Directions:

Pretend that you're a dog stretching to lick his paw.

1. Sit on the floor, legs stretched out, back straight.
2. Bend your left leg and, keeping the side of the knee on the floor, bring your left foot against the right thigh, close to the body. INHALE. (Figure 25)
3. Stretching the arms up, EXHALE and slide them SLOWLY down your right leg as far as you can reach, bending forward with a curling motion of the spine.
4. Grasp the leg; this may be at the knee, calf or ankle, depending on your flexibility. (Figure 26)
5. Bend the elbows out and down, and gently pull yourself forward rather than down. Let your head hang loosely. Avoid strain by making this a smooth, not jerky, motion.
6. Go only as far as you comfortably can and then hold the position 5-30 seconds. Breathe normally.
7. INHALE, straighten up slowly and repeat on the other side.
8. Perform three times on each side.

Dos and Don'ts:

DON'T bend your knees and don't jerk. It is the motionless holding of the Yoga positions that does the most effective work and prevents strain.

DO use your leg as a lever by grasping it tightly and pulling yourself forward on it.

DO loosen the knees by alternately banging them against the floor when you've finished the pose.

DON'T feel discouraged if you're not nearly so close to your knee as your friend. The beauty of Yoga is that *if you stick with it* you progress very fast.

Benefits:

THE ALTERNATE LEG STRETCH

•strengthens and firms the abdomen and leg •massages most abdominal organs and stimulates them into action •makes the spine supple and strong •reduces tension from the legs, buttocks and back.

(Figure 25) Good starting position.

(Figure 26) Beginners should go only as far as comfort permits.

(Figure 27) Advanced pose.

CAMEL

Directions:

Pretend you are a camel trying to bring his head to his hump.

1. Kneel in an upright position, keeping the legs together, toes pointed back. INHALE.
2. Place hands on the waist and bend slowly backward, EXHALING and pushing the hips forward. (Figure 28)
3. Let the head hang back.
4. Let the right hand hang down over the heel, then the left, and put palms on the feet, if possible. (Figure 29)
5. Pinch the buttocks together, pushing the thighs and hips well forward. (Figure 30)
6. Hold this position for as long as possible or from 5-30 seconds. Breathe normally. (Figure 30)
7. Repeat twice more.

Dos and Don'ts:

DO remember to keep the chest and hips thrust forward for a better bend.
DON'T press beyond the point of comfort.
DO keep your mouth shut—it's good for the chin.

Benefits:

THE CAMEL

•makes the spine flexible and tones it •gives a feeling of energy •improves posture •benefits rounded shoulders and hunched backs •beneficial to people with spinal injuries, because it is so gentle.

(Figure 28) Starting position.

(Figure 29) A beginner needn't go further.

(Figure 30) Advanced pose.

(Figure 31) Needs much practice.

31

COBRA

Directions:

Pretend to be a Cobra slowly uncoiling after a sleep in his basket.
1. Lie on your stomach, hands by your side, feet together.
2. Bring the hands, palms down under the shoulders, a shoulder's width apart.
3. INHALE and perform a Cobra, bringing the head back and arching the spine as far as it will go—can you see the ceiling?
4. Keep the thighs firmly pressed against the floor; the arms need not be straight. Tighten the buttocks and thighs. Then relax in the pose. (Figure 32)

Variations:
1. Repeat Steps 1 to 4.
2. EXHALE. Bend the knees and attempt to bring the toes to the head. (The advanced pose is called the Swan.) (Figure 33)
3. Hold the pose 5-15 seconds, breathing normally.
4. Slowly relax, EXHALING. Repeat twice more.

Dos and Don'ts:

DO think of the spine as a heavy chain and raise this chain slowly, link by link.
DO bring the head up first and let it come down last.
DO give a good stretch to the legs and the body in this position.
DON'T force any position that doesn't come easily.

Benefits:

COBRA

•expands the chest and develops the bust •is beneficial to lumbar, dorsal and sacroiliac areas of the spine •massages and reduces fat in the abdominal area •strengthens the wrists •tightens the chin area •acts as a great vitalizer •stretches and relieves tension in the shoulders and neck •corrects urinary problems •improves the circulation to the pelvic area.

(Figure 32) Cobra for beginners to work towards.

(Figure 33) Tanya is showing the swan.

(Figure 34) Cobra on toes — keep knees and elbows locked.

33

FISH

Directions:

Pretend to be a shark swimming on his back ready to take a nip at a swimmer.

1. Lie on your back, legs outstretched, arms by your sides, palms down. IN-HALE. (Figure 35)
2. EXHALE, push down on the elbows and raise your chest off the floor, really arching the back.
3. At the same time pull your head under until you are resting on the very top of it or as close as you can get to the crown. (Figure 36)
4. Shift most of your weight over to the bottom.
5. Hold the position for 5-60 seconds or until you start to be uncomfortable. Breathe normally.
6. INHALE, slowly come out of the pose and repeat twice more.

Variations: (Figures 37, 38)

Dos and Don'ts:

DO put most of your body weight onto the bottom and elbows.
DON'T bend your legs at all.
DO the Fish right after any pose that puts strain on the neck.
DO practice the Fish in the lotus position.

Benefits:

THE FISH

•develops the chest and bust line •exercises the hip joints •is beneficial for asthma and other respiratory complaints •stimulates the thyroid gland for weight control •limbers up and relieves tension in the neck and upper back •improves circulation to the head: for a wide-awake and alert feeling •aids digestion •relieves painful piles.

34

(Figure 35) Starting position.

(Figure 36) Basic beginner's pose.

(Figure 37) Try the legs
in a Lotus position.

(Figure 38) Excellent for
the tummy.

FORWARD BEND
STANDING

Directions:

Pretend to be an ostrich trying to get the head so low that he can hide it in the sand.

1. Stand, with the feet slightly apart.
2. Raise your hands slowly, INHALING. (Figure 39)
3. EXHALE and slowly bend forward from the waist in a curling motion, dropping your head first. (Figure 40)
4. Keeping your arms beside your ears, let your body hang forward by its own weight for a few seconds. (Figure 40)
5. Grasp the back of your ankles, or whatever you can comfortably reach, without bending your knees and dig your chin into the neck. (Figure 41)
6. Bend your elbows to the side and give a gentle downward and inward stretch, *attempting* to get your head to the knees.
7. Hold for 5-30 seconds, breathing normally.
8. Straighten up slowly, INHALING and keep the arms beside the ears; curling the spine up.
9. Repeat twice more.

Variations: (Figures 42, 43)

Dos and Don'ts:

DON'T bounce or jerk in order to bring your head closer to your knees.
DON'T worry how close your hands are from the floor. Rather think how far your head is from your knees.
DON'T EVER bend your knees, in order to go farther.
DO hang just by your body weight at first, to loosen up the tight hamstring muscles.

Benefits:

FORWARD BEND STANDING

•removes tension from the back and shoulders •releases tension in the hamstring muscles and makes the legs flexible •improves circulation to the head, working on complexion, as well as giving a feeling of alertness •limbers up the spine •helps to reduce excess fat •aids digestion and elimination.

(Figure 40) Beginners can just hang by their body weight.

(Figure 39) Keep those knees straight!

(Figure 41) Advanced position.

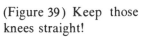

(Figure 42) Two fingers around the big toe.

(Figure 43)

37

FORWARD BEND SITTING

Directions:

Pretend to be the anchorman in a sitting tug-of-war whose team has nearly lost.

1. Sit on the floor, legs stretched out, feet together and back straight.
2. INHALE, raise your arms above your head and lean back slightly. (Figure 44)
3. EXHALE, breath out and slowly bend forward with a curling motion of the spine; when you have reached your limit without straining or bouncing, grasp tight that part of your legs which you can reach.
4. Now bend the elbows and pull the body forward and down. (Figure 45)
5. Let your head hang and hold the pose for 5 to 30 seconds, breathing normally.
6. Eventually you will be able to bring your head to your knees and grasp the toes instead of the ankles by bringing the elbows to the floor. (Figure 46)
7. INHALE, return slowly out of the pose and repeat twice more.

Dos and Don'ts:

DO keep your knees straight.
DO *NOT* bounce to go further. This can cause injury.
DO concentrate on giving a good stretch to the spine.

Benefits:

FORWARD BEND SITTING

•strengthens the abdominal muscles and tones the abdominal organs •limbers up and releases tension in legs and spine •gives a feeling of vitality •stretches the pelvic region and improves the circulation there •is beneficial to the entire nervous system •tones the kidneys •massages the heart.

(Figure 44) Lean slightly back.

(Figure 45) Pull smoothly, no jerking.

(Figure 46) Keep stretching, it can be done.

FOUNTAIN

Directions:

Pretend that you're a fountain with your fingers as the spout. Round and round you sprinkle in an ever-widening circle.

1. Stand, feet slightly apart, hands clasped in front of you.
2. INHALE and slowly raise the clasped hands over your head and bend as far back from the waist as you can manage. Hold for a few seconds. EXHALE. (Figure 47)
3. INHALE and continue to describe an ever widening circle with your body from the waist up by first bending to the left, to the front, and then to the right, stopping, holding for a few seconds and EXHALING at each location. (Figure 48 and Figure 49)
4. Relax and repeat counter-clockwise. Breathe normally throughout. Repeat twice more in each direction.

Variations:

a) Perform the same steps as above but come up on your toes and balance throughout.
b) Perform the Fountain without stopping but in slow motion in one IN-HALATION.
c) Increase the size of the circles you describe with your body.

Dos and Don'ts:

DO keep your bottom tucked in when you are bending to the sides and to the back.
DON'T bend your knees or move your feet.
DO make it a round, not an oval, circle; don't avoid the back.

Benefits:

THE FOUNTAIN

•tightens and reduces weight in the hips •reduces waist •stretches entire side of the body •improves circulation in the arms •relieves tension.

40

(Figure 47) Starting
position of the larger circles.

(Figure 48) Good for
losing spare tires.

(Figure 49) Now we go
forward to complete the
circle.

41

LION

Directions:

Pretend that you're a lion cub sticking out your tongue to show Poppa how HUNGRY you are.

1. Sit in a kneeling position, placing the hands on the thighs, palms down. (Figure 50)
2. Spread the fingers and slide them forward till tips touch the floor.
3. Bend your body forward, bottom off the heels, arms straight.
4. Open your eyes as wide as possible.
5. Stick your tongue out as far as it will go, attempting to touch the tip of your chin. (Figure 51)
6. Hold 10 seconds.
7. Sit back, pull in your tongue and relax completely.
8. Repeat twice more.

Dos and Don'ts:

DO stick your tongue out completely for a good stretch.

DON'T be surprised if you have a gagging sensation for awhile.

DO the Lion facing the sun with the eyes closed.

DO enjoy the marvellous feeling of tension draining away when you sit back.

DO make your Lion act convincing; maybe you would rather pretend you were angry.

Benefits:

THE LION

•tightens and firms the muscles of the face, neck and throat •smoothes lines and wrinkles •relieves a sore throat and improves the voice •improves the circulation and complexion •reduces a double chin •reduces tension in the face area.

(Figure 50) Starting
position.

(Figure 51) Stick out
your tongue — further,
further!

43

POSTURE CLASP OR COW HEAD POSE

Directions:

Pretend to be a cow who is reaching up to scratch behind the ear.

1. Sit in a comfortably cross-legged position, back straight.
2. Bring your left hand behind your back, palm facing out and try to wriggle it up your back as far as it will go. (Figure 52)
3. Lift your right hand straight up and bend it at the elbow, bringing the hand to the center of the back. This pose got its name because of the elbow sticking up to look like a horn. (Figure 53)
4. Try to get the two hands close enough together to interlock with the fingers, by gently inching them together.
5. Hold the position for 10-30 seconds and try a gentle upward pull with the right hand, then a downward pull with the left. (Figure 53)
6. Repeat on the other side and twice more on both sides.
7. You will find that one side is much more flexible than the other. Concentrate on the stiffer one.

Dos and Don'ts:

DO keep your back straight and you will have better success.
DO use a kerchief or book if you just can't bring the two hands together.
DO that pose right behind your desk when you feel uptight after hours of study.
DO bend forward for an extra good stretch.

Benefits:

THE COW HEAD POSE/THE POSTURE CLASP

•improves posture and rounded shoulders •firms and strengthens the upper arms •tones the leg muscles •exercises muscles around shoulder blades and upper back •removes leg cramps •improves circulation to the head •eases tension in the shoulders •oils the shoulder joints (eases arthritis).

44

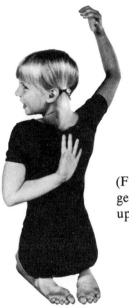

(Figure 52) Starting position: get the arm high up the back.

(Figure 53) Use kerchief or ruler if fingers don't reach.

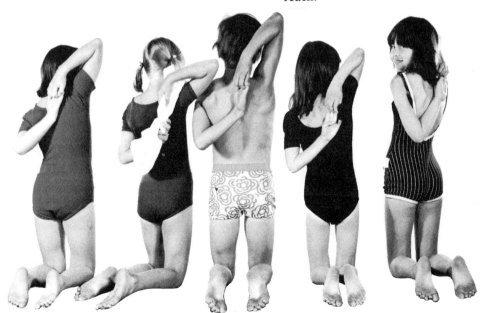

45

TREE OR STORK

Directions:

Pretend that you're a stork standing in your snug nest on top of a high chimney.

1. Stand with your feet together, arms by your side.
2. Bend the right leg and prop the sole of the foot against the left thigh.
3. Eventually bring the heel as close to the groin as possible with the help of your hands and rest the foot there, pointing the knee to the side. (Figure 54)
4. Bring the palms together and raise the hands straight over the head.
5. Hold as long as balance permits and breathe deeply.
6. Lower the leg and hands slowly and relax.
7. Repeat with the left leg.
8. Repeat twice more on both sides.
9. For the Stork variation, simply bend one knee, bringing the heel up to the bottom, with the arms out to the side. (Figure 55)

Dos and Don'ts:

DO prop your foot slightly to the front of the thigh for better support. It has a tendency to slide if too far back.

DO practice your balancing first, if necessary, by keeping arms out to the sides.

DON'T come out of the pose suddenly.

DO become a hopping, wing-flapping stork after holding the pose motionless for as long as you can.

DO practice your balance, while on the phone, washing dishes or waiting for a green light.

Benefits:

THE TREE / THE STORK

•promotes poise and grace through improving balance •teaches proper posture since the body must be perfectly aligned to keep balance •tones the leg muscles •improves circulation in lower extremities.

46

(Figure 54) The Tree. Stre-e-e-etch out or over-head.

(Figure 55) The Stork. Close your eyes and balance.

47

TRIANGLE POSTURE

Directions:

Pretend to be a penguin doing a cartwheel.

1. Stand with the feet 3 feet apart.
2. INHALE and bring your arms out straight at the sides, parallel to the floor. (Figure 56)
3. Point your right foot at a 90° angle, the left foot slightly to the right.
4. EXHALE and bend your body to the left, bringing the hand as close as possible to the outside of the left calf. (Figure 57)
5. Bring your right arm up so that it is in a straight line with the left arm. Look up at the right hand.(Figure 58)
6. Hold 10-30 seconds, breathing normally. INHALE and come up slowly.
7. Repeat on the other side; then twice more on each side.

Variation:

1. Do steps 1 to 3 as above.
2. With arms out-stretched, twist your body to the right and bring the left arm as close as possible to the outside of the right foot.
3. Bring your right arm up in line with the left arm. Look at the right arm. (Figure 59)
4. Complete stages 6 and 7 as above.

Dos and Don'ts:

DO keep your knees absolutely straight throughout. It is not so important how far you go as that you do it properly.

DO stretch your shoulders as you hold.

DO keep in mind that yoga has such a relaxing effect because unlike calisthenics it has a holding position. Try both ways and see the difference.

Benefits:

THE TRIANGLE POSTURE

•develops chest •tones hip, thigh and leg muscles • relieves backache •relieves menstrual problems •massages and stimulates abdominal organs.

(Figure 56) Starting position.

(Figure 57) Don't lose the benefits by pushing the bottom out.

(Figure 58)

(Figure 59) One hand goes to the opposite toe; look up at the other.

49

INTERMEDIATE KEEP FIT YOGA POSES

This is the next step after Easy Keep Fit Poses.

Simple Variations should now
be tried by beginners.

Don't forget to warm up before
you do any poses.

Have you checked what benefits
you get from each exercise?

THE ANKLE TO FOREHEAD
STRETCH

Directions:

Pretend you are a monkey who wants to scratch behind the ear with his foot.

1. Sit, legs outstretched.
2. Bend the right leg bringing the foot close to the body, letting the knee fall to the side.
3. From underneath grasp the right foot around the ankle with the right hand (or vice versa).
4. Get a good grasp around the ball of the foot with the left hand. (Figure 60)
5. EXHALE, raise the foot as high as you can or on a level with the face.
6. Pull the ankle to the forehead or as close as possible. (Figure 61)
7. Hold the pose for 5-30 seconds, breathing normally. EXHALE, relax.
8. Repeat on the other side.

Variation: (Figure 62)

Dos and Don'ts:

DO bend your trunk forward at first to get the ankle and the forehead together. Straighten the trunk as you improve.
DO keep the other leg straight.
DON'T attempt any variations until you can do the Ankle to Forehead Stretch.
DO enjoy the delightful stretching feeling to the whole hip region.

Benefits:

THE ANKLE TO FOREHEAD STRETCH

•stretches and firms the thighs and hip muscles •strengthens the arms •raises a "slipped hip" (works on the fatty lower hip) •is beneficial to the hip joints •massages the abdominal organs and improves digestion •relieves sciatica.

(Figure 60) Starting position.

(Figure 61) Up she goes!

(Figure 62) Ankle be-
hind the head. How's the
itch?

BOW

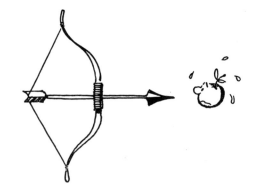

Directions:

Pretend that you are a bow whose string is getting tightened by Robin Hood.

1. Lie face down on your tummy, hands by your side.
2. EXHALE, bend your knees and bring them close to your bottom.
3. Grasp your legs at the ankles, one at a time; take two breaths. (Figure 63)
4. EXHALE, lift your knees off the floor by pulling the ankles *away* from the hands. You will still be tightly holding on, but it is the *away* motion rather than a *down* pull that will do the trick.
5. Lift your head at the same time. (Figure 64)
6. Hold the position for 5-10 seconds at the first, increasing to 30 seconds at 5 seconds a week. Breathe normally.
7. EXHALE slowly, relax and rest for awhile.
8. Repeat twice more.

Variations: (Figures 65, 66, 67)

Dos and Don'ts:

DO come out of the exercise slowly.
DO pull the ankles "up and away" rather than down to get those stubborn knees off the ground.
DON'T collapse in a heap. You will get more exercise for your time.
DO get a little rocking motion going by breathing deeply — it'll help pass the time.
DO use scarves around the ankles if you can't reach them because you are over-weight or very stiff.

Benefits:

THE BOW

•relieves pain from a slipped disc •tones and firms the muscles of the abdomen, arms, legs, and back •develops and firms the muscles of the chest and bustline •strengthens and limbers up the spine •reduces weight in hips and buttocks •aids digestion •improves posture.

(Figure 63) Starting position.

(Figure 64) Push those ankles away.

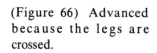

(Figure 65) Easy Bow with one foot — also called Cobra-Bow.

(Figure 66) Advanced because the legs are crossed.

(Figure 67) Bow to the Side — get up first, then tip over.

CROW

Directions:

Pretend you are a crow dipping down its beak to get a drink of water.

1. Squat on the heels, feet about half a foot apart.
2. With the arms against the inside of the knees, rise onto the toes and bend slightly forward.
3. Place the hands on the floor in front of you, the thumbs about 6″ apart, the fingers spread and slightly pointed towards each other.
4. Now press the area of the arms just above the elbow against the side of the knee. (Figure 68)
5. Breathe out, bend forward, bringing the face closer to the floor and gently lift the toes off, pressing the elbows against the knees.
6. Try to straighten the arms as much as possible and balance on the hands, breathing normally for 5-20 seconds.
7. EXHALE, lower the toes and relax. Repeat twice more.

Variation: (Figure 69)

Dos and Don'ts:

DO use a pillow on the floor in front of your face to give you confidence.

DO keep the toes of one foot poised to help you with your balance.

DO be sure to press the area just above the elbows against the side of the knee just above the fleshy part.

DO bring the bottom off the heels, and the face close to the floor before you lift the toes.

DO remember that the Crow is a balancing pose and as such requires more confidence than skill.

DO practice the pose with the top of your head on the floor at first. (Figure 70)

Benefits:

THE CROW

•strengthens and firms abdomen •promotes balance and poise •strengthens the neck without undue pressure •strengthens and develops the pectoral muscles of the bust-line •strengthens arms and wrists •acts as a preparation to the Headstand.

55

(Figure 68) Three steps at the same time.

(Figure 69) Try a variation.

(Figure 70) Put your head down and go over into a Forward Roll when you're getting tired.

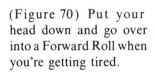

KNEE AND THIGH STRETCH

Directions:

Pretend you are on a magic carpet.

1. Sit on the floor, legs outstretched, back straight.
2. Bend your knees to the side and bring the soles of your feet together. (Figure 71)
3. Clasp your fingers tightly around the toes and gently pull the feet as close to the body as you can. (Figure 72)
4. Now with a great effort of will, widen the thighs and attempt to bring the knees to the floor by pulling up on the toes. (Figure 73) The arms and back should be straight.
5. Hold the position for as long as you can — from 5-30 seconds. The secret here lies in breathing normally as you are holding.
6. Relax by stretching the legs out and shaking them if you wish.
7. Repeat twice more or 4 times if you are really concerned about your health problem or flabby inner thighs.

Dos and Don'ts:

DO clasp your fingers tightly around the toes to give you a good hold and to prevent slipping.

DO keep your back straight.

DON'T push the knees forcibly with your hands. You can accomplish much more by your will.

DON'T be discouraged if your knees look like craggy mountains for awhile. By trying often you have an excellent chance of eventually laying the knees on the floor.

DO try to relax, even as you are holding.

Benefits:

THE KNEE AND THIGH STRETCH

•firms and reduces weight in inner thighs •gives new vitality to tired legs •stimulates function of the ovaries and helps to regulate menstrual periods •is very beneficial for bladder and urinary problems •relieves sciatic pain.

57

(Figure 71) Toes together.

(Figure 72) Pull the heels as close as you can.

(Figure 73) Pull up on the toes.

58

LOCUST (BOAT)

Directions:

Pretend to be a locust flinging up his legs in a jump.

1. Lie on your stomach, hands by your side, palms up.
2. Raise your head and place the front of the chin on the floor.
3. Make fists of your hands and place them under the thighs in the groin.
4. For beginners — raise one leg as high as it will go. (Figure 75)
5. Repeat with the other leg.
6. INHALE, stiffen the body and pushing down on the arms bring the legs up in back, as high as they will go. (Figure 76)
7. Hold the pose for 5-10 seconds, holding the breath as well.
8. EXHALE, lower the legs slowly and relax. Rest for awhile.

Boat Variation: (Figure 74)

Dos and Don'ts:

DO practice the Half-Locust only, for several weeks, to strengthen a weak back. (Figure 75)
DO put all your energy and concentration on your arms and legs as you inhale in preparation for the Locust.
DO press your chin firmly into the ground.
DO try to make your knees as straight as possible.
DON'T kick up with a thrust, but rely on your strength. How *far* you go up is not important.
DO use great pressure on the arms to get the legs up.
DO come out of the pose slowly, so as not to lose a third of the benefit.
DON'T roll over to the side or come up on the knee in order to bring the leg up further.

Benefits:

THE LOCUST (BOAT)

•firms the buttocks •firms and reduces weight in the hips •tightens and flattens the abdomen •relieves pain in the sacral and lumbar areas of the back •is beneficial to people with a slipped disc •aids digestion •is beneficial to the bladder and gonads.

(Figure 74) Boat, arms
and legs are up.

(Figure 75) Beginner's
Half-Locust.

(Figure 76) This variation
needs much practice.

LOTUS (Perfect Posture)

Directions:

Pretend to be a famous Guru speaking of peace.

1. Sit with both legs extended and spread apart.
2. Bring the sole of the right foot against the thigh of the left leg, resting the right knee on the floor.
3. Bend the left leg and gently lift the left foot onto the right foot.
4. Put the ankles beside each other. Snuggle the toes of the left foot between the thigh and calf of the right leg. (Figure 77)
5. Keep your spine straight and try to keep both knees as close to the floor as possible.
6. Rest in this position until the beginning of discomfort.
7. Change feet and try again.

Variations:

HALF-LOTUS

1. Repeat steps 1 to 2 as above.
3. Bend the left leg and clasp the left foot, around the outside edge, with both hands and gently lift it onto the right thigh, as high up and as close to the groin as possible.
4. Straighten the spine and relax. (Figure 78)

FULL LOTUS

1. Repeat 1 to 3 of the Half-Lotus.
4. Now slightly lift the left knee and slide the right foot out from under it.
5. Clasp the right foot around the outside edge with both hands and gently lift it onto the left thigh as close to the groin as possible.
6. Straighten the spine and relax. (Figure 79)

Benefits:

LOTUS (PERFECT POSTURE)

•stretches and tones legs and lower back •is relaxing for the entire body •is ideal for prolonged sitting •is beneficial to bladder and urinary tracts.

61

(Figure 77) Perfect Posture:
a very comfortable
sitting position.

(Figure 78) Half-Lotus:
it's good enough for be-
ginners and inter-
mediates.

(Figure 79) Full Lotus:
it's mainly for meditating.

Dos and Don'ts:

DON'T force the feet into a higher position than comfort allows.

DO take your time — some can do the Lotus immediately others need a year of practice.

DON'T rush because the muscles of the knee are easily strained.

DO keep trying. While just sitting you are exercising.

PLOW

Directions:

Pretend that you are a plow being pulled by its handles (your feet).

1. Lie on your back on the floor, legs outstretched, arms extended by your side, palms down.
2. EXHALE and slowly lift your legs by tightening the stomach and leg muscles, pushing the curve in the back against the floor.
3. EXHALE, *push down on your hands,* making them hollow or tent-like and raise your bottom and lower back. Beginners can bend the knee. Take two breaths. (Figure 80)
4. Bring your legs over your head, attempting to touch the floor behind you with the toes, by bending at the waist. Keep your knees straight. (Figure 82)
5. Stretch the toes away from the body.
6. Hold the position, even if your feet are nowhere near the floor, for as long as you comfortably can or up to a minute.
7. Breathe normally.
8. Slowly come out of the pose by bending your knees, but straighten the legs when they are pointing at the ceiling.

Variations: (Figures 81, 83)

Dos and Don'ts:

DON'T become discouraged if you can only raise your bottom a couple of inches off the floor. Simply go as far as you can, hold it there and repeat this action several times. The holding process strengthens and prepares the proper muscles for the exercise.

DO keep your knees straight throughout.

DON'T lift your head as you lower your legs.

DO breathe normally. It will get easier with practice.

DO place your legs on a low bench behind you if you feel choked.

Benefits:

THE PLOW

•makes the spine supple •stimulates the thyroid gland for weight control •strengthens and firms the abdomen •slims and firms thighs and hips •acts as an energy pick-me-up •strengthens the neck •massages such abdominal organs as the liver, spleen, pancreas and kidneys •improves circulation •tones up the nervous system •relieves deep-seated tension and headaches.

63

(Figure 80) Beginning position: push down hard on the hands.

(Figure 81) Turn the wrists until the thumbs are on the floor.

(Figure 82) The proper Plow pose: point the toes and stretch.

(Figure 83) Fingers pointing toward the shoulders, push down for Backward Roll.

REVERSE ARCH

Directions:

Pretend to be an overpass over a railway track.

1. Lie on your back, knees bent, feet flat on the floor, arms by your side.
2. Pull the feet as close to the buttocks as possible, without straining.
3. Exhale and slowly tilt the pelvis up, pushing the small of the back (the hollow) against the floor. The pelvis is NOT lifted, only tilted.
4. Hold the pose, exhale and lower the pelvis. Repeat once more.
5. Now, inhale and slowly push the buttocks and lower body up as high as you can. (Figure 84)
6. Shift the weight towards the shoulders, relax the arms, and breathe normally.
7. Hold 5-30 seconds. Exhale and relax slowly, bringing the back down vertebra by vertebra. Repeat three to four times.

Variation 1:

1. Repeat steps 1-6.
2. Now, stretch one leg forward. Hold. Relax. (Figure 85)

Variation 2:

1. Repeat steps 1-6.
2. Now, come up on your toes and take a step towards the buttocks. Hold. Relax.

Dos and Don'ts:

DO only *tilt* the pelvis without lifting it, in steps 1-4. The buttocks should not be wholly off the floor. The feeling should almost be one of pinching the buttocks together.

DON'T keep the weight on the arms. Shift the weight to the shoulders and relax the arms as much as possible.

DO enjoy the delightful stretching sensation in your upper legs.

Benefits:

REVERSE ARCH

● relieves menstrual pain ● exercises and firms the hips, buttocks and legs ● strengthens the sacroiliac region of the back ● relieves backache.

(Figure 84) Really push up the pelvis.

(Figure 85) Stretch the pointing leg.

SHOULDERSTAND (CANDLE)

Directions:

*Pretend you are a straight candle and the toes
are a flickering flame.*

1. Lie on the floor, legs outstretched, hands close by your side, palms down.
2. EXHALE and slowly lift your legs by tightening the tummy and leg muscles, until they are pointing at the ceiling.
3. Press down on your hands, making them hollow or tent-like. Take 2 breaths.
4. EXHALE, raise your bottom and lower back and grab yourself around the waist, with the thumbs around the front of the body. DO NOT let the elbows stick out. This is a Half Shoulderstand. (Figure 86)
5. Straighten the legs and tuck the bottom in as much as you can.
6. If you are balancing well, then grasp yourself higher up on the rib-cage. (Figure 87)
7. Stretch your legs and point your toes. Hold the position from 10-60 seconds, as a beginner. Gradually work up to 3 minutes. Breathe normally throughout.
8. Try some variations with your feet and hands after your balance is good. (Figures 88 to 94)

Dos and Don'ts:

DO tuck your bottom in for a straighter look as you advance.

DO stretch your toes up.

DON'T get alarmed if you feel slightly dizzy or heady at first. It is quite normal and can be blamed on the sudden dilation of the blood vessels. (Note to girls: inverted poses should not be practiced during menstruation.)

DO be patient with yourself. The important thing is to be up there at all, even if it is only a Half-Shoulderstand for some time. That is better than doing a full Shoulderstand badly.

Benefits:

THE SHOULDERSTAND

•is a cure-all for most common ailments •improves the circulation to such important areas as the brain, the spine, the pelvic area; these are areas which, due to an upright position, rarely receive a good supply of rich, newly-oxygenated blood •presses the chin against the thyroid gland which stimulates it and reduces excess fat •tones up the central nervous system and soothes it (tension, insomnia) and is a marvellous rejuvenator •has a beneficial effect on the hormone-producing glands of the body •relieves pressure on abdominal organs due to body-inversion, which, in turn, regulates the digestive processes, frees the body of toxins and increases the energy-level •is beneficial for urinary disorders and menstrual troubles and piles •relieves varicose veins and aching legs •gives new vitality to people who suffer from anemia or lack of energy •relaxes the whole body •stretches the spine •strengthens and firms the muscles of the back, legs, neck and abdomen.

(Figure 86) (Figure 87) (Figure 88)

(Figure 89) (Figure 90) (Figure 91)

(Figure 92) (Figure 93) (Figure 94)

TWIST

Directions:

Pretend that you are teaching your pet to do the Twist.

1. Sit on the floor, legs outstretched.
2. Spread your legs and bring the right foot against the left thigh. Press the side of the right knee against the floor. (Figure 95)
3. Bend your left knee and, leaving it sticking up in the air bring the left foot over the right knee.
4. Set the sole of the left foot squarely on the floor. The further back you can bring the foot, the better.
5. Using both hands for support, shift your weight well forward, to prevent tipping.
6. With the left hand behind you on the floor for support raise your right arm and bring it between your chest and the left knee. (Figure 96) (If the left leg sticks up, *both* hands go to the left and vice versa.)
7. EXHALE and twist your body slightly forward so that your right shoulder is resting against the left knee. Take two breaths. (Figure 96)
8. Now make a fist of your right hand, EXHALE and move your right arm poker-straight over the right knee that is lying on the floor. (Figure 97)
9. Attempt to get hold of the toes of the left foot. As a beginner, that is nearly impossible, so it is perfectly all right to grasp the right knee. (Figure 97)
10. Levering yourself against the left leg with the right arm, now twist to the left.
11. EXHALE, bend your left arm and bring the back of the hand around your back. (Figure 98)
12. Turn your head to the left and look as far left as you can. (Figure 99)
13. Hold this position for 10-30 seconds.
14. Slowly unwind.
15. Repeat on the other side.

Dos and Don'ts:

DO sit well forward.

DON'T bend your arm as you draw it across the knee.

DO turn your shoulder or upper arm against the knee to permit you to bring your arm around further.

DON'T get discouraged with this complicated looking pose. Just study the photographs carefully.

Benefits:

THE TWIST

•tones muscles and firms figure •makes spine limber which has a therapeutic effect on the nervous system •makes the hip flexible •firms and reduces waist •realigns vertebrae and relieves tension.

(Figure 95) Starting position.

(Figure 96) The left leg is up, so both arms go to the left.

(Figure 97) "Junior" twist.

(Figure 98) The full twist — hand behind the back.

(Figure 99) Keep the foot of the upright knee as far back as possible.

WARRIOR (Sitting and Reclining)

Directions:

Pretend that you are a knight in shining, but heavy, armour sitting down for a rest.

Sitting Warrior

1. Kneel in an upright position, knees together, the feet a bottom's width apart. (Figure 100)
2. Slowly lower your body to sit between the feet on the floor. Use your hands for support on your way down at first.
3. Straighten your back and keep the toes pointed straight back. (Figure 101)

Reclining Warrior

1. Now EXHALE, lean back and bring your elbows to the floor one by one.
2. Let your head hang back and slowly straighten the arms (clasping the ankles if you wish), shifting the weight onto the top of the head.
3. As you improve, lower the head completely until you are comfortably resting on the shoulders and the back of the head.
4. Stretch the arms straight over the head and hold the pose from a few seconds to 10 seconds eventually, breathing deeply. Very advanced. (Figure 102)
5. EXHALE, grab the ankles, dig the elbows in and sit up. Relax.

Dos and Don'ts:

DO relax in the pose. It is marvellously resting after awhile.

DO keep your knees apart at first, to permit full execution of the pose.

DO just place the hands beside the thighs if stretching them over the head proves difficult.

DO NOT give up if sitting with the feet apart is difficult at first. Cross your ankles for awhile and sit on the feet this way. Gradually move your feet farther and farther apart.

DO NOT force the Reclining Warrior position without being comfortable in the Sitting Warrior first.

Benefits:

THE WARRIOR

•stretches and makes shapely the thighs and legs •relieves aching legs if done for ten minutes •is beneficial for flat feet •eases breathing for asthma sufferers •relieves rheumatic pain in the knees and heels •keeps genital organs healthy •tones and stretches the abdominal and pelvic area.

(Figure 100) Starting pose.

(Figure 101) Sitting Warrior.

(Figure 102) Reclining Warrior.

(Figure 103) Very Advanced — head to toe backwards.

ADVANCED KEEP FIT
HATHA YOGA POSES

Try these poses only if:
you have done a warmup and if
you have mastered the
Intermediate Poses.

Variations are only for the
advanced unless you try the
poses carefully and slowly.

HEADSTAND WALK-UP/ HEADSTAND

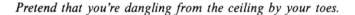

Directions:

Pretend that you're dangling from the ceiling by your toes.

Headstand Walk-up

1. Make sure that you have adequate support for your head: a carpet with underfelt or a blanket folded in four.
2. Kneel on the carpet or in front of the blanket, with your toes tucked under.
3. Now place your tightly clasped hands on the floor, a shoulder's width apart. This is measured by bringing the span of your hand between the thumb and index finger against the elbow bend of the other arm.
4. Place the very top of the head on the floor, disregarding the hands for now.
5. Now pull the folded hands against the back of the head on the floor. The little fingers will be under the head.
6. Tuck the toes under and push your bottom straight up, and with the knees absolutely straight throughout, slowly tippy-toe up towards your head. Make the back straight. (Figure 104)
7. When you can go no further, hold the position for as long as comfort permits, then slowly walk down again. The Headstand Walk-Up should end with a Curling Leaf relaxation.

Headstand begins

8. When the toes lift off without pushing, in the Headstand Walk-Up (and only then), bend your knees and bring the heels to the buttocks. EXHALE. (Figure 105)
9. Balance in this position until you are secure, then *SLOWLY* straighten out the legs.
10. Tuck your bottom in and try to get the body into a completely straight line. (Figure 106)
11. Hold this position from 10 seconds to 5 minutes, increasing your time by a minute a week or according to your ability.
12. Slowly return the legs to the floor by bending the knees and reversing the getting-up process.
13. When you have mastered a one-minute Headstand, you might try some leg and hand variations. (Figures 107 to 111)

(Figure 104) Tippy-toe with the knees straight.

(Figure 105) Hold it for a minute before trying to bring the legs up.

(Figure 106) That's the Headstand — as straight as can be.

Dos and Don'ts:

DO clasp your hands very tightly and take your rings off to prevent slipping and undue strain on the arms.

DON'T let your elbows flare out or press against the head. For a perfect tripod they are a shoulder's width apart.

DO put the crown of the head on the floor. It is not the hairline nor the back of the head that will support you longest and most comfortably. Eventually you may be able to stand on your head from 5-30 minutes.

DON'T put the back of the head against the hands but rather bring the hands against the head. Do a little nestling there to make sure you are comfortable.

DO keep the knees very straight to make possible a straight back.

DON'T, repeat DO NOT, push up on your toes to get you up into the Headstand. Unless the toes lift off by themselves you are not ready to bring the legs up. Even when you are ready, practice balance by hugging the knees to the chest for awhile. The hardest part of the Headstand is bringing the legs up and that is mainly done by strong tummy muscles. The Headstand is a feat of strength rather than skill.

DO practice the Cobra and the Bow to make the neck strong and flexible. This is especially true of round-shouldered people.

DO take your time and be patient with yourself. The Headstand is one of the most difficult poses in Yoga and will take time, strength, flexibility and balance to accomplish. Develop these skills first.

DO try the Headstand in the corner of a room, about 2″ from the wall. A partner who grasps the ankle of the first leg to go up and the second leg on the way down, will give you extra courage, too.

Benefits:

HEADSTAND

•circulation is greatly improved to areas which normally get little: i) brain, ii) heart, iii) pelvis, iv) spinal cord •the nervous system is toned owing to balancing and circulation •abdominal organs, which normally sag or prolapse, are pulled into original position •stomach muscles are firmed and strengthened •sinus fluids are now permitted to flow downward •the endocrine, pituitary and pineal glands are stimulated into normal action •energy and a general feeling of alertness are experienced •strengthens the lungs •digestion and elimination are improved •the following ailments are removed or their condition is improved: a) insomnia and nerves; b) colds and sore throats; c) palpitations; d) bad breath; e) headaches; f) asthma; g) varicose veins.

(Figure 107) The Un-Yoga Headstand: because you cannot stay up too long.

(Figure 108) Try this variation.

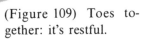

(Figure 109) Toes together: it's restful.

(Figure 110) The Lotus was done while already on the head.

(Figure 111) The Leg-Split upside-down.

LEG SPLIT

Directions:

Pretend that you are taking your first ballet lesson.

1. Squat on your toes.
2. Place the hands, a shoulder's width apart, on the floor in front of the toes.
3. Slide the left leg forward, straightening the knee as much as possible. (Figure 112)
4. Now, EXHALE, shift your weight forward onto the hands, lift the bottom and slide the right leg backward.
5. At the same time keep sliding the left leg forward to make a straight line of the legs.
6. Press the groin slowly towards the floor, letting the hands take most of the weight. (Figure 113)
7. Once you can sit completely on the floor (and this will take much practice) raise the hands, and bring them together in front of the chest or try to raise them over your head and balance on the legs. (Figure 114)
8. Hold this position for 10-30 seconds, breathing normally.
9. With the help of the hands, return to the squatting position, sit down and relax. Repeat on the other side.

Dos and Don'ts:

DON'T, repeat DO NOT, force the groin towards the floor. Let time and your body weight do the work, even if it takes months!

DO concentrate on keeping the legs straight, the heel of the forward leg and the upper part of the backward foot resting on the floor.

DO let your hands support your weight at first, only gradually settling on the groin.

DO remember that it takes a ballerina years to perfect this position. Just the attempt will really exercise both legs.

Benefits:

THE LEG SPLIT

•promotes dancer's flexibility and poise •firms and strengthens the thigh •tones and makes shapely the whole leg •exercises the hip joint •helps to cure sciatica.

78

(Figure 112) Starting position.

(Figure 113) Try to sit on the groin.

(Figure 114) Have good balance before trying.

79

PEACOCK

Directions:

Pretend to be a wooing peacock.

1. Kneel, knees slightly apart, toes tucked under.
2. Bend forward and place the hands, with fingers pointing back towards the body, close together on the floor. Press the elbows together, the little fingers touching.
3. Bend the elbows and press them against the body (near the diaphragm), resting the chest on the upper arms. The face will be close to the floor.
4. Straighten the legs out in back one by one, resting on the top of the feet, the feet together.
5. EXHALE, shift your weight onto the hands and stretch forward, slowly raising the legs in back.
6. Hold this position from 5-30 seconds, breathing hard. Increase your holding time gradually over a matter of weeks. (Figure 116)
7. EXHALE, slowly lower the body to the floor, head first and relax for some time.
8. Repeat, even if you only hold it for a short time.

Dos and Don'ts:

DO use a pillow in front of your face to give you confidence at first.

DO practice other wrist and arm-strengthening poses such as the Crow, Cobra, Wheel, etc. if you find you have little strength.

DO remember to stretch the body forward, shifting your weight onto the wrists and hands.

DO keep the feet together, and the elbows, the forearms and the little fingers touching.

DON'T feel bad if you're a girl and just can't do the pose — it's a real power-pose. (Figure 115)

Benefits:

THE PEACOCK

•develops arms and shoulders •strengthens the wrist, lower arm and elbow • gives a marvellous massage to the abdominal organs •improves the circulation there and therefore relieves all sorts of stomach complaints •improves digestion and elimination •is recommended for people with diabetes •rids the body of accumulated toxins (poisons).

80

(Figure 115) The fingers point towards the legs.

(Figure 116) Go up slowly, do not force.

SPIDER

Directions:

Pretend to be a spider having a hard time building her web.

1. Lie on your back, the legs extended.
2. Place the left hand on the left thigh, bend the right knee and hug it to the chest.
3. Grab the right foot under the toes. (Figure 117)
4. EXHALE, and slowly lift the head, at the same time straightening the right knee and bringing it to the head.
5. Keep the leg straight and pull the leg as much as you can, attempting to touch it with the head. (Figure 118)
6. Hold for 5-20 seconds, breathing normally.
7. INHALE, lower the body and relax.

Variation: (Figure 119)

Dos and Don'ts:

DO keep the outstretched leg absolutely straight and on the floor throughout.
DO keep the hand on the outstretched leg.
DO remember it is more important to keep the leg straight than to bring the head to the knee.
DO wrap the thumb and index finger around the big toe if you find it's more effective for you.
DO try to bring the outstretched leg to the floor on the side, if you are advanced.

Did you know that the Spider is called Padangusthasana which really means Lying Down Foot Big Toe pose?

Benefits:

THE SPIDER

•tightens and firms the hips and thighs •limbers up the hip joints •improves circulation and tones the legs •prevents hernia •is an excellent exercise for people with paralyzed legs •relieves the pain of sciatica.

(Figure 117) Starting position.

(Figure 118) A variation of a Head to Knee pose.

(Figure 119) The leg comes up first, then the knee is bent.

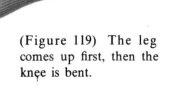

83

TORTOISE

Directions:

Pretend that you're a tortoise hiding under its shell.

1. Sit on the floor, the legs about 2 feet apart.
2. Bend the knees up slightly, pulling the heels a few inches closer to the body.
3. EXHALE, bend forward and from the inside slide the right arm under the bent right knee, then the left arm under the left knee.
4. Push the arms through sideways as much as possible, bringing the shoulders and the head to the floor. (Figure 120)
5. When you can go no further, push the knees down, straightening the legs.
6. Hold this position for 10-60 seconds, breathing normally.

Variations: (Figures 121, 122)

Dos and Don'ts:

DO stretch the arms and neck forward for a perfect pose.
DO attempt to bring the chest and the front of the face to the floor eventually.
DON'T spread the legs too wide.
DO have the arms palms down when they are out to the side, and palms up when you bring them around the back.
DO treat the Tortoise with respect — it's a very advanced pose.

Benefits:

THE TORTOISE

•stretches most muscles of the body which has a relaxing effect •stretches and tones the spine and legs •stimulates and tones the abdominal organs •gives a feeling of energy •stimulates the glands and kidneys.

84

(Figure 120) Knees
down, palms down.

(Figure 121) Arms
around the back.

(Figure 122) Cross your
feet.

WHEEL

Directions:

Pretend you are a flat tire about to be blown up.

1. Lie on your back, legs outstretched, arms by your side.
2. Bend both knees and bring the heels as close to the bottom as possible, toes pointing to the side.
3. Grab the ankles with the hands and pull the heels even closer, keeping them about 1½ feet apart.
4. Bring the hands forward, up and over, placing them on the floor beside the head, a shoulder's width apart, THE FINGERS POINTING TOWARDS THE SHOULDERS. (Figure 123)
5. EXHALE, push down on the hands and raise the body, resting the top of the head on the floor. Take a few normal breaths.
6. EXHALE and arch the back, lifting the whole body and shifting the weight to the hands and feet.
7. Stretch the hips up and straighten the arms and legs as much as possible.
8. Hold, breathing normally, from 10-60 seconds. (Figure 124)
9. EXHALE, slowly lower the body and relax.
10. Try some advanced variations.(Figures 125, 126 & 127)

Dos and Don'ts:

DO come up on your toes after step 7 of the original Wheel. This will give an extra good arch to the spine. Then, without collapsing the arch, slowly lower the heels to the floor.

DO place a small pillow on the floor behind your heels to give you confidence.

DO keep your head completely bent back, the eyes looking up in their sockets.

DO tighten the thighs for a good arch.

DON'T come up on your toes during step 5.

DON'T attempt any pose that is beyond your ability without strengthening THE MUSCLES INVOLVED first.

Benefits:

THE WHEEL

•stretches the spine completely and makes the body supple •is a great energizer •has a flattening effect on the abdomen •firms the thighs •develops the pectoral muscles of the bustline •has a tightening effect on the buttocks •strengthens arms and wrists •expands the chest for easier breathing •improves circulation to the head and has a soothing effect.

(Figure 123) Starting position.

(Figure 124) The Wheel.

(Figure 125) A Wheel from a handstand position.

(Figure 126) Shift your weight onto the left leg and lift the right.

(Figure 127)   Wheel against the wall.

This exercise is good for practicing to get up and down from a standing position.

RELAXATION POSES

After each workout (or even
after each pose) relax to
let your body remember what
it has learned as you rest.

If you don't need to rest
yet, try another pose or two
even if you repeat yourself
in your personal schedule.

Relaxing means letting go,
melting into the carpet,
floating on a cloud. It
means that you don't worry,
watch TV, read a book or
even sleep. You simply
relax, think of nothing and
try to be absolutely quiet.

Remember that your mind
becomes more efficient after
you have relaxed it.

CURLING LEAF

(Figure 128)

Directions:

Pretend to make yourself into a very small ball.

1. Kneel with legs together.
2. Rest your bottom on the heels and the top of your hands on the floor, pointing back.
3. Lower your head slowly to the floor, the hands sliding gently back palms up, to lie beside the body. (Figure 128)
4. Rest your head on the floor and relax completely with the chest against the knees.
5. Hold for any length of time, the longer the better.

Dos and Don'ts:

DO the Curling Leaf any time you need a rest or pick-up.

DON'T stick your bottom up in the air but put your whole weight on your legs and heels.

DO remember that the Curling Leaf is also called "The Pose of a Child" because it is the same position a baby is in before being born. That's why it is so natural and relaxing.

Benefits:

THE CURLING LEAF

•eases tension, is wonderfully relaxing •improves circulation to the head which benefits the complexion •acts as an energy pick-up •beneficial to tired legs and spider veins.

90

SPONGE

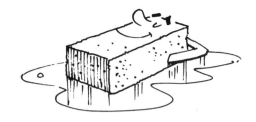

Directions:

Pretend to be a Sponge lying in a puddle of relaxation. Soak it up quietly, without effort.

1. Lie on the floor, legs slightly apart, arms limply by your side. (Figure 129)
2. Now point your toes away from you and hold for 5 seconds, really stretching. Relax.
3. Pull the toes up towards the body, bending at the ankle. Hold. Relax.
4. Pull your heels up two inches on the floor and then straighten the legs, pushing the back of the knees firmly against the floor. Hold. Relax.
5. Point the toes toward each other and pull the heels under and up, keeping the legs straight. Hold. Relax.
6. Pinch your buttocks together. Hold. Relax.
7. Pull your tummy in and up as far as possible. Hold. Relax.
8. Arch the spine back, pushing the chest out. Hold. Relax.
9. With arms straight by your side, palms down, bend the fingers up and back toward the arm, bending at the wrist. Hold. Relax.
10. Bend the elbows and repeat step 9, bending the hands back toward the shoulders. Hold. Relax.
11. Make a tight fist of your hands, bring the arms out to the sides and move the arms up from the floor. Move very slowly resisting the movement all the while to make the chest muscles of the bust stand out. Let the arms fall.
12. Pull the shoulderblades of the back together. Hold. Relax.
13. Pull the shoulders up beside the ears. Hold. Relax.
14. Pull down the corners of the mouth. Hold. Relax.
15. Bring the tongue to the back of the roof of the mouth. Hold. Relax.
16. Purse your lips, wrinkle your nose and squeeze the eyes tightly shut. Hold. Relax.
17. Smile with the lips closed and stretch the face. Hold. Relax.
18. Yawn very slowly, resisting the movement.
19. Press the back of the head against the floor. Hold. Relax.
20. Frown, moving the scalp forward. Hold. Relax.
21. Go through the eye exercises.
22. Pull your head under and against the shoulders without moving anything else.
23. Relax, melting into the floor for up to 10 minutes.
24. Or go through all the relaxing steps once more without moving a muscle. Simply tell each part of the body to relax, then rest.

(Figure 129)

Dos and Don'ts:

DO hold each holding position for at least 5 seconds and really work on stretching or tightening the muscles.

DO relax after each holding position, by flopping back into place.

DON'T worry or think of unpleasant things as you relax at the end of the
sponge. If you must think, rather keep your thoughts on pleasant things,
and watch them wander past without trying to become involved. Think of
peace.

DO remember that once your body has really learned the pose, you won't have
to go through all these steps anymore in order to relax.

Benefits:

THE SPONGE

•promotes deep muscular relaxation •deeply relaxes the nervous system • is a marvellous energy-
recharger •results in a reduction of anxiety or "nerves" through the release of tension •restores
peace of mind.

BREATHING

Most people use only
1/5 of their lung-power

Do you?

You can't live long without breathing, so learn to do it correctly.

COMPLETE BREATH

Directions:

*Pretend that you are a sailor after he has swallowed
his can of spinach: expand your chest.*

1. Sit in a comfortably cross-legged position or in a straight-backed chair.
2. Straighten your back, which will straighten your throat for easier breathing. Exhale.
3. Inhale slowly through the nose, breathing deeply, concentrating on the in and out flow of your breath.
4. Take five seconds to fill the lower part of the lungs, by expanding the ribs and pushing the tummy out.
5. Concentrate on filling first the middle then the top of the lungs for the next five seconds. This will expand the chest and tighten the abdomen slightly.
6. Hold the breath for 1-5 seconds, by either bringing your chin down to your chest or pretending to swallow.
7. Exhale slowly through the nose, tightening the tummy muscles and even bending slightly forward if you like.
8. Repeat 4-5 times more.

Dos and Don'ts:

DO establish a rhythmic rise and fall of your abdomen, to promote regular breathing. To establish accurate rhythm you could feel your pulse with one hand.

DO attempt to breathe without much noise after you have gotten the knack of deep breathing. The ingoing breath should have a slight sssssssss-sound, the outgoing one should sound like hhhhhhhha.

DON'T slump.

DO concentrate on your breathing alone, with your eyes closed, if you wish.

DO push your abdomen *out* as you breathe *in* and pull the abdomen *in* as you breathe *out.*

DO give an extra snort as you exhale to rid yourself of stale waste-matter in the bottom of the lungs.

DO always exhale before starting your first breath.

Oxygen is our most important food and the customary shallow breathing of most people can be compared to the hasty swallowing of food: both cause health problems. If you regularly breathe deeply you can improve your digestion and your general health and have a great deal more energy.

(Figure 130)

COOLING BREATH

Directions:

Pretend you are hiding underwater breathing through a reed.

1. Sit comfortably in a cross-legged position, back straight.
2. Form your tongue into a trough and let it protrude slightly from the lips. Use a pencil or little finger to make your tongue round. (Figure 130)
3. Inhale air through this trough with a hissing sound.
4. Hold your breath for 1-5 seconds.
5. Exhale through the nostrils, pulling tummy muscles in.
6. Repeat 5 more times.

Dos and Don'ts:

DO this breath before you are ill, so that you know how to do it when you get a fever.

DON'T inhale too forcefully, but make it a steady, slow pull, expanding the chest and abdomen.

95

INDEX